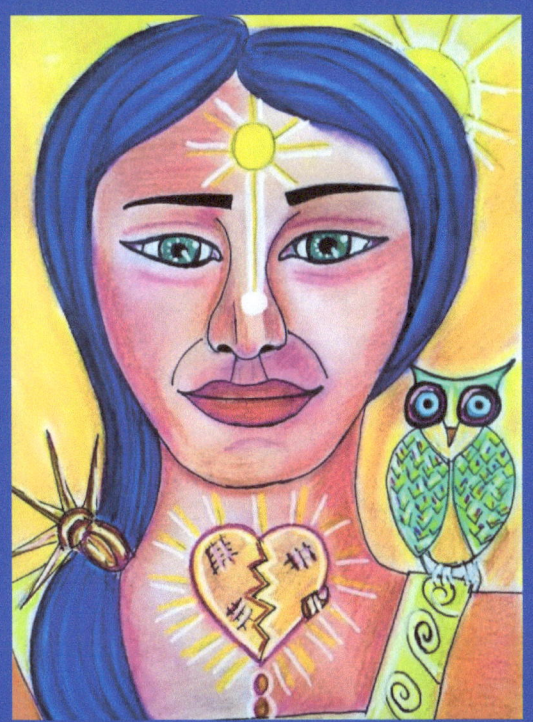 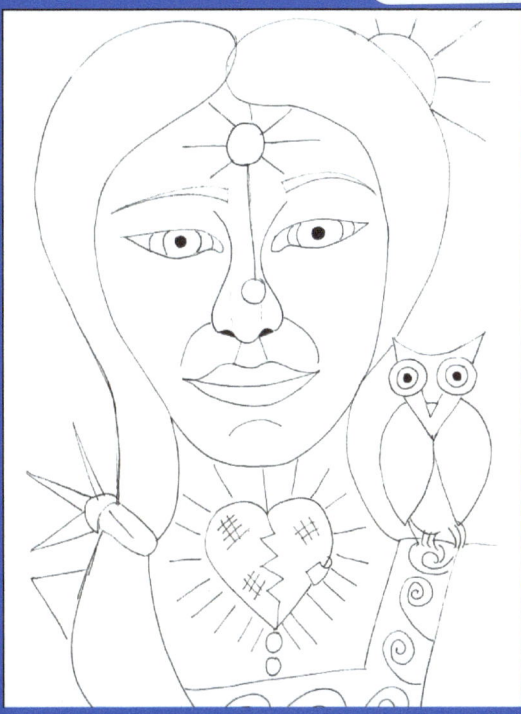

Spiritual Guides Colouring Book

By Alessandra Del Basso

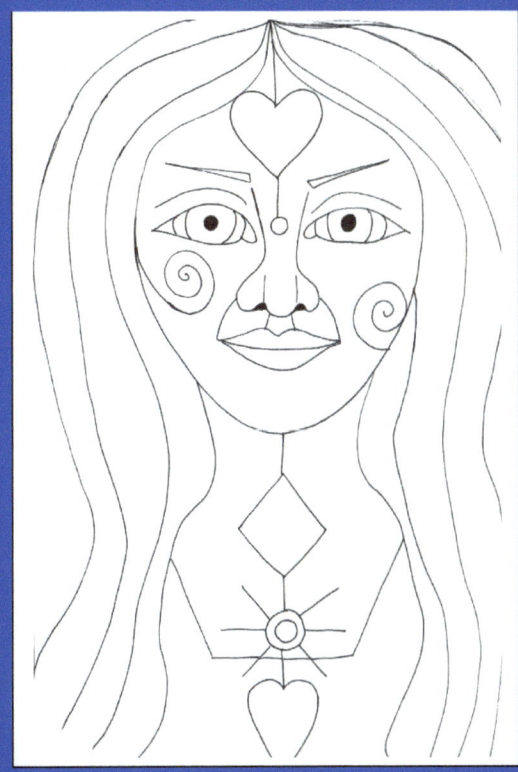 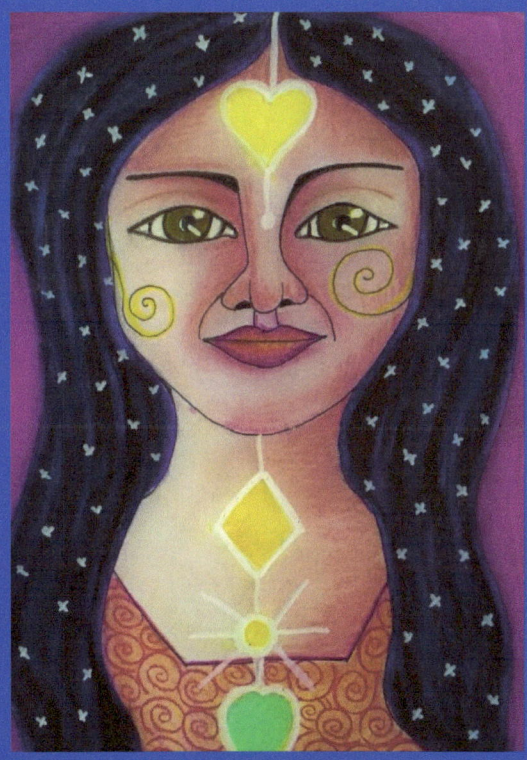

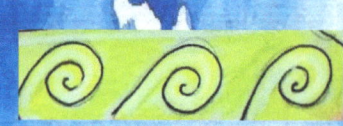

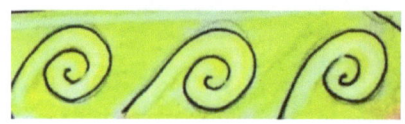

When there is no enemy within, the enemies
outside cannot hurt you [African proverb]

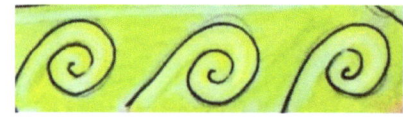

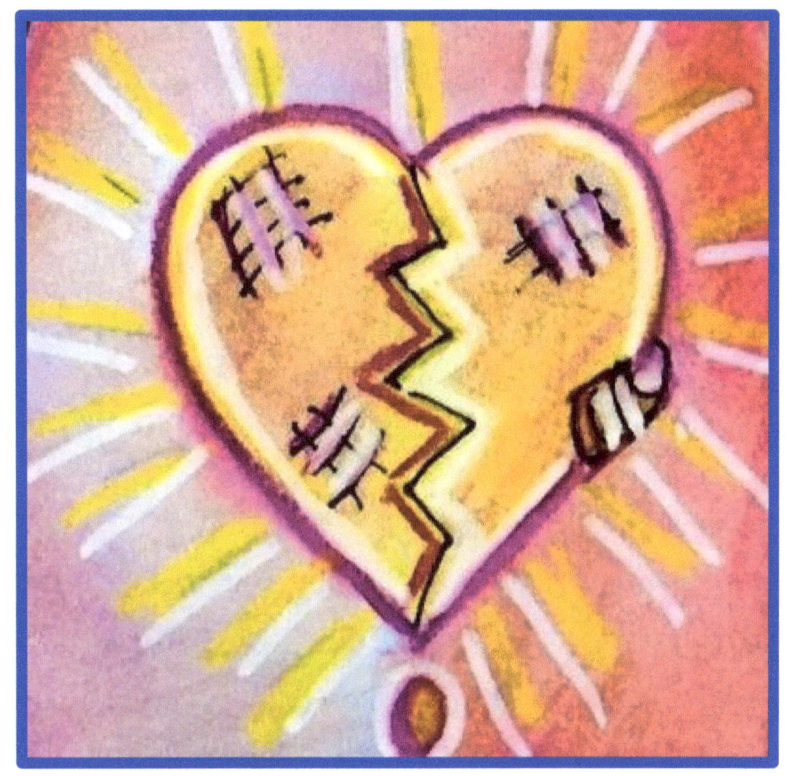

This Colouring Book belongs to:

....

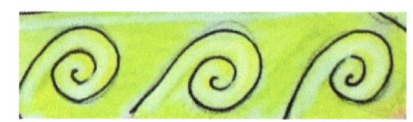

Introduction

This "Spiritual Colouring Book" derives from my own drawings and paintings used for the Journals {see Amazon or innersilence7@gmail.com to request a catalogue).I hope you too will enjoy colouring in the pages and are inspired to create your own. Everything is possible "when you believe".

Luv and Light Alessandra

P.S. Have Fun Creating your own on the blank pages

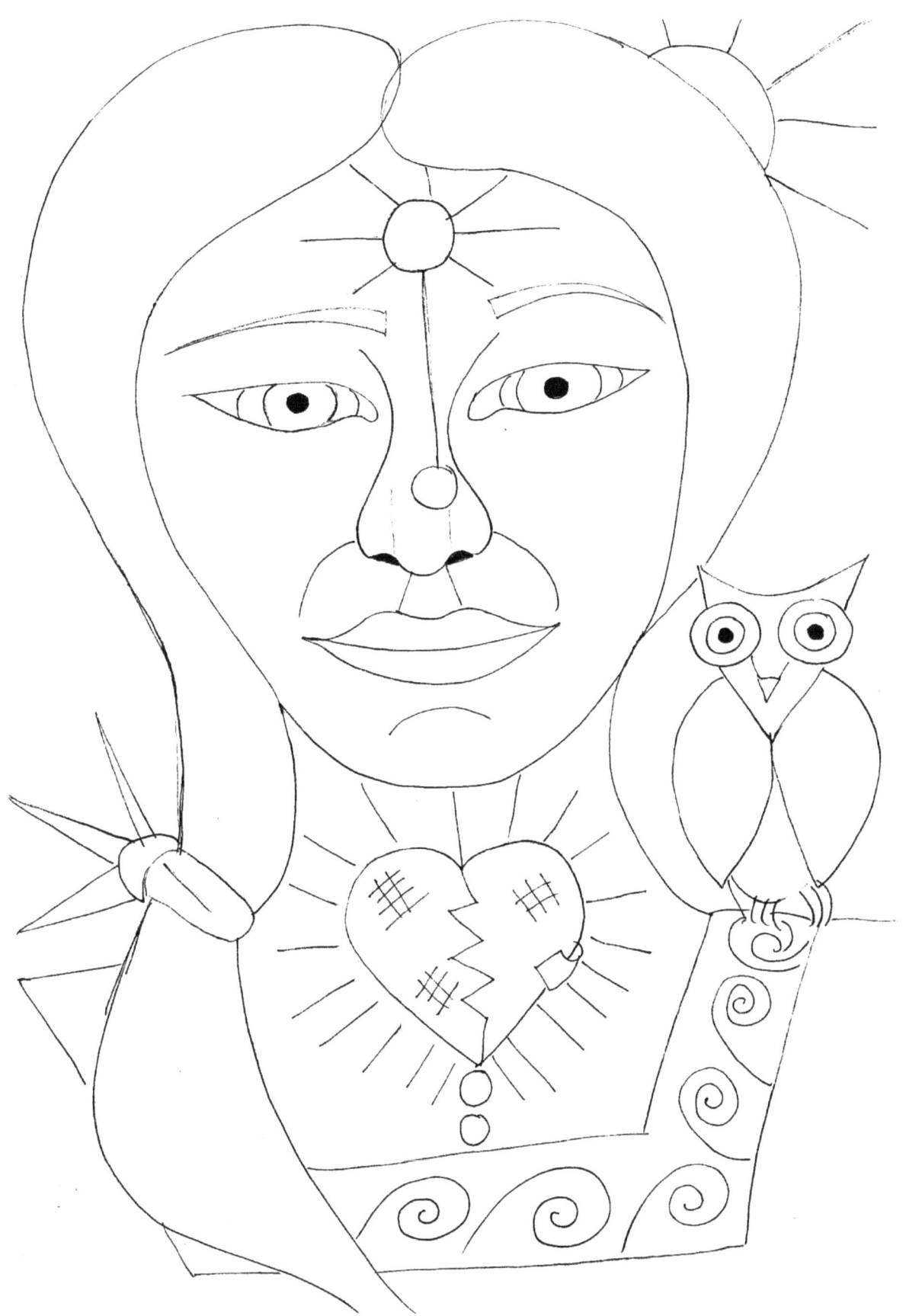

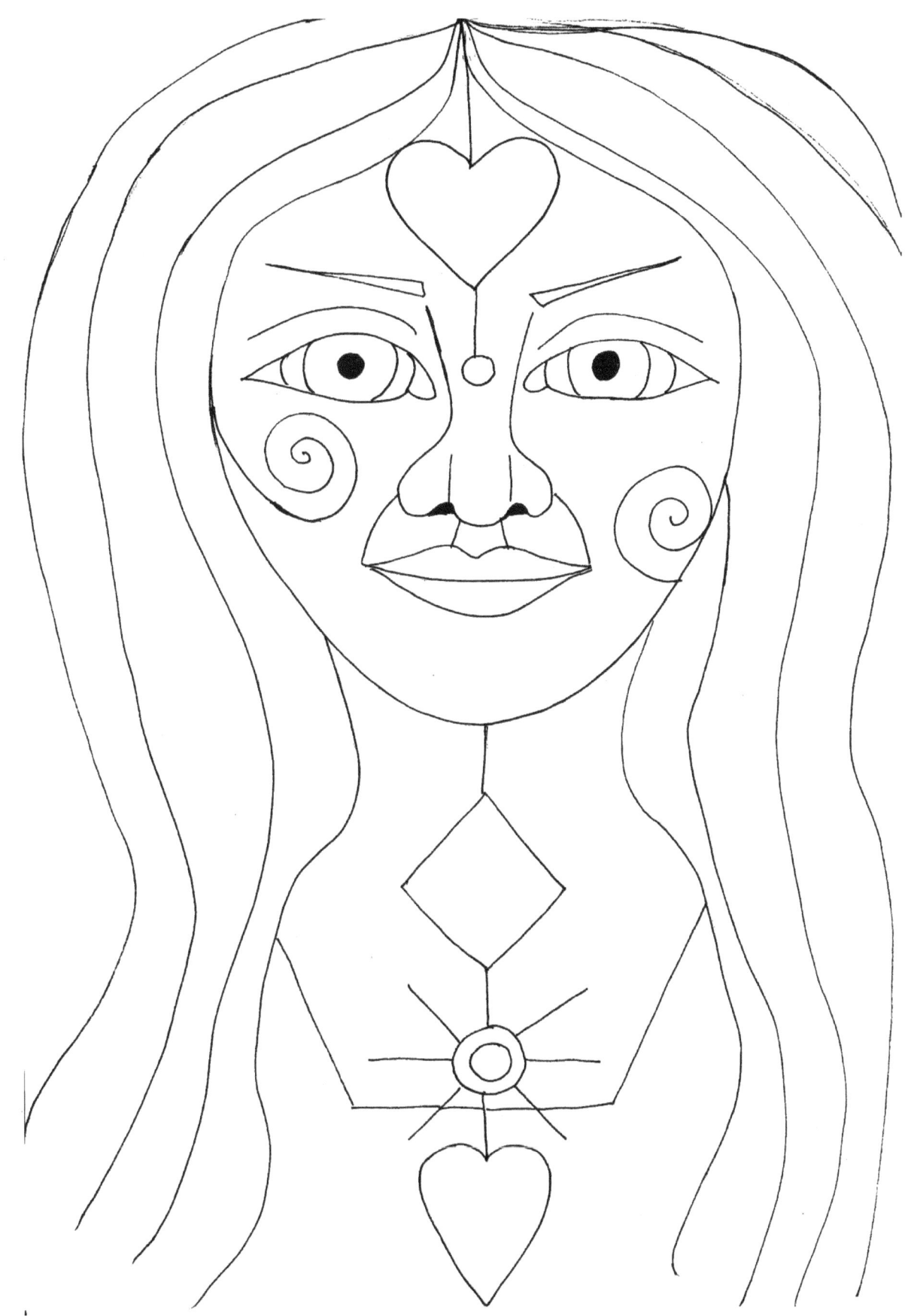

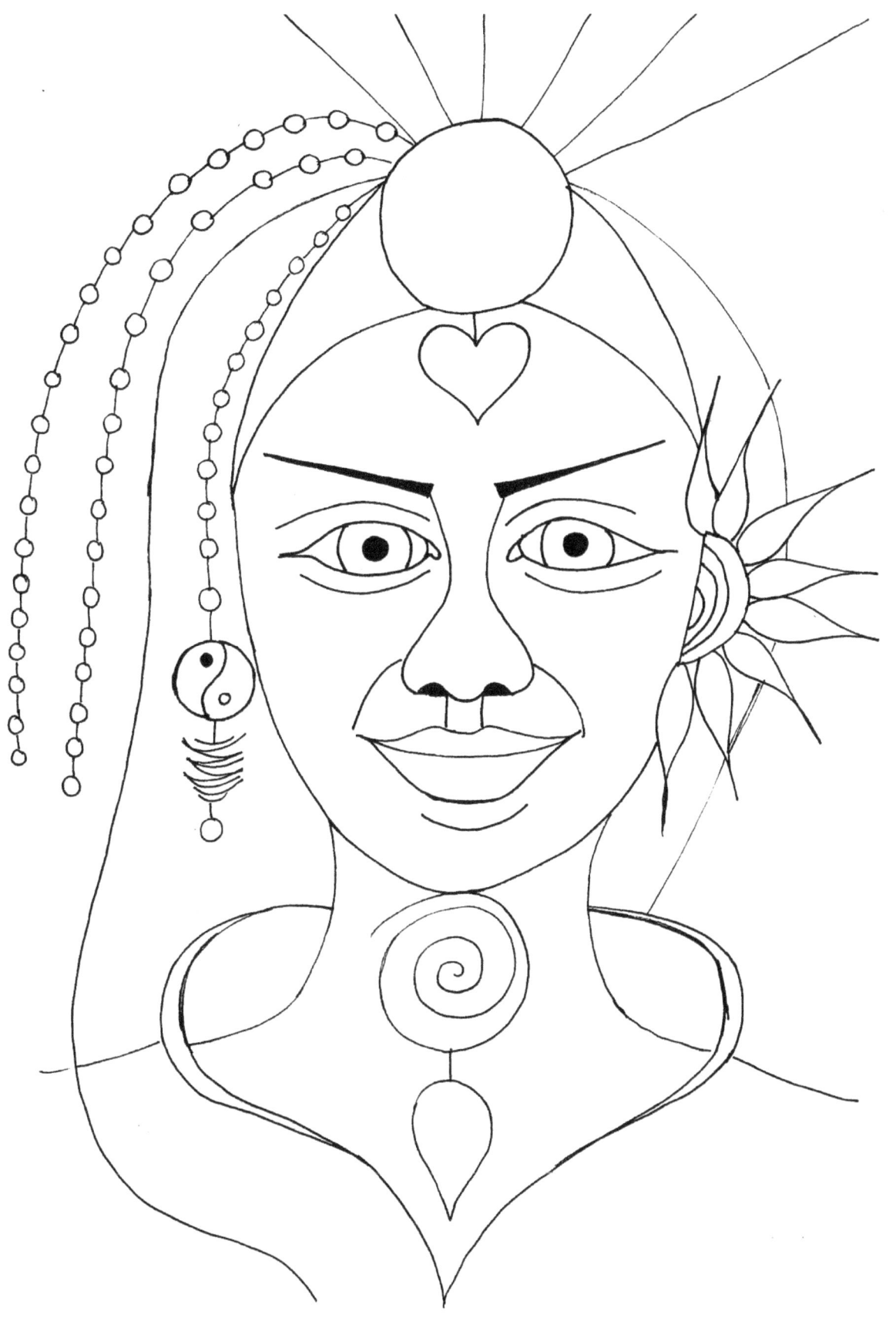

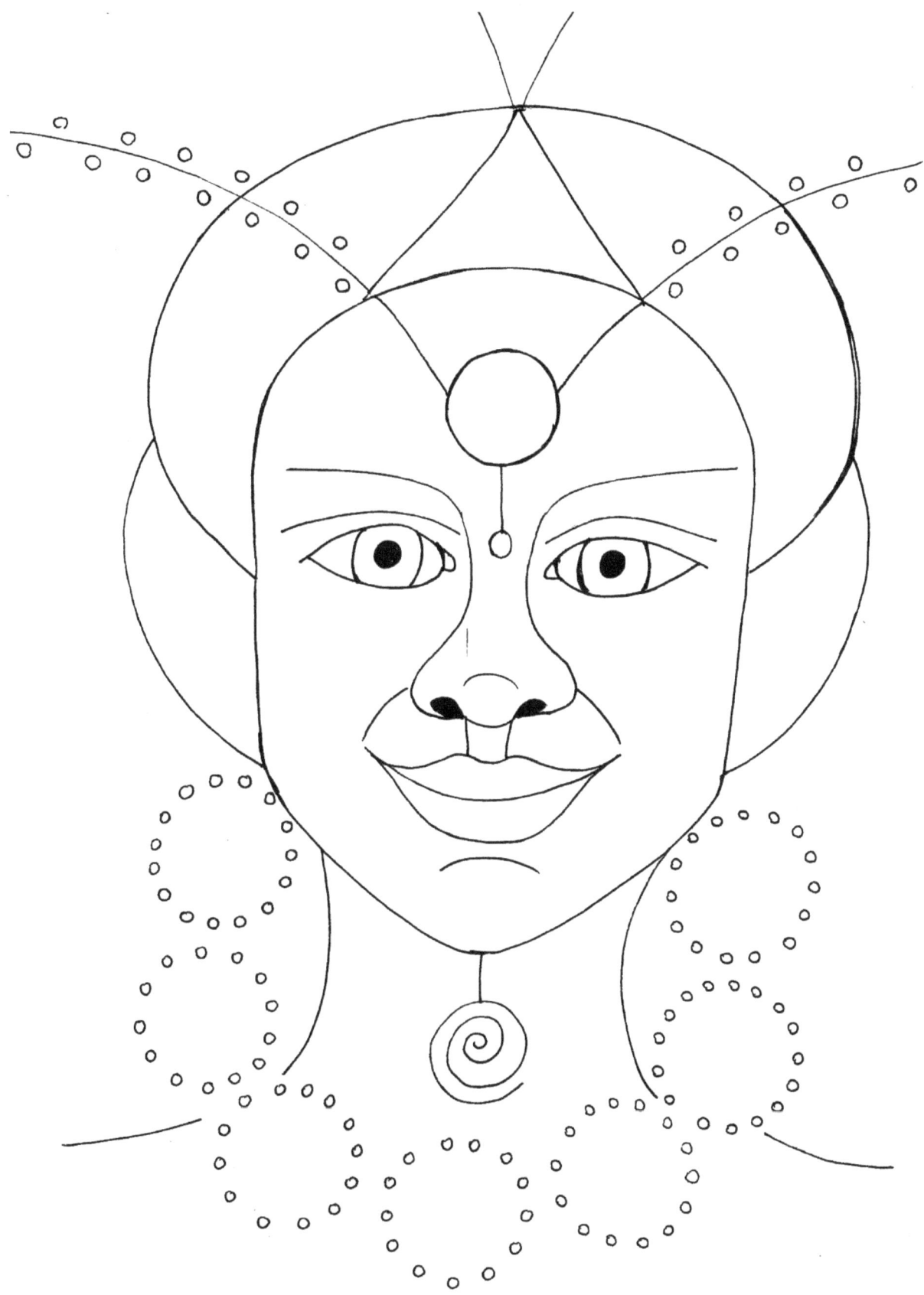

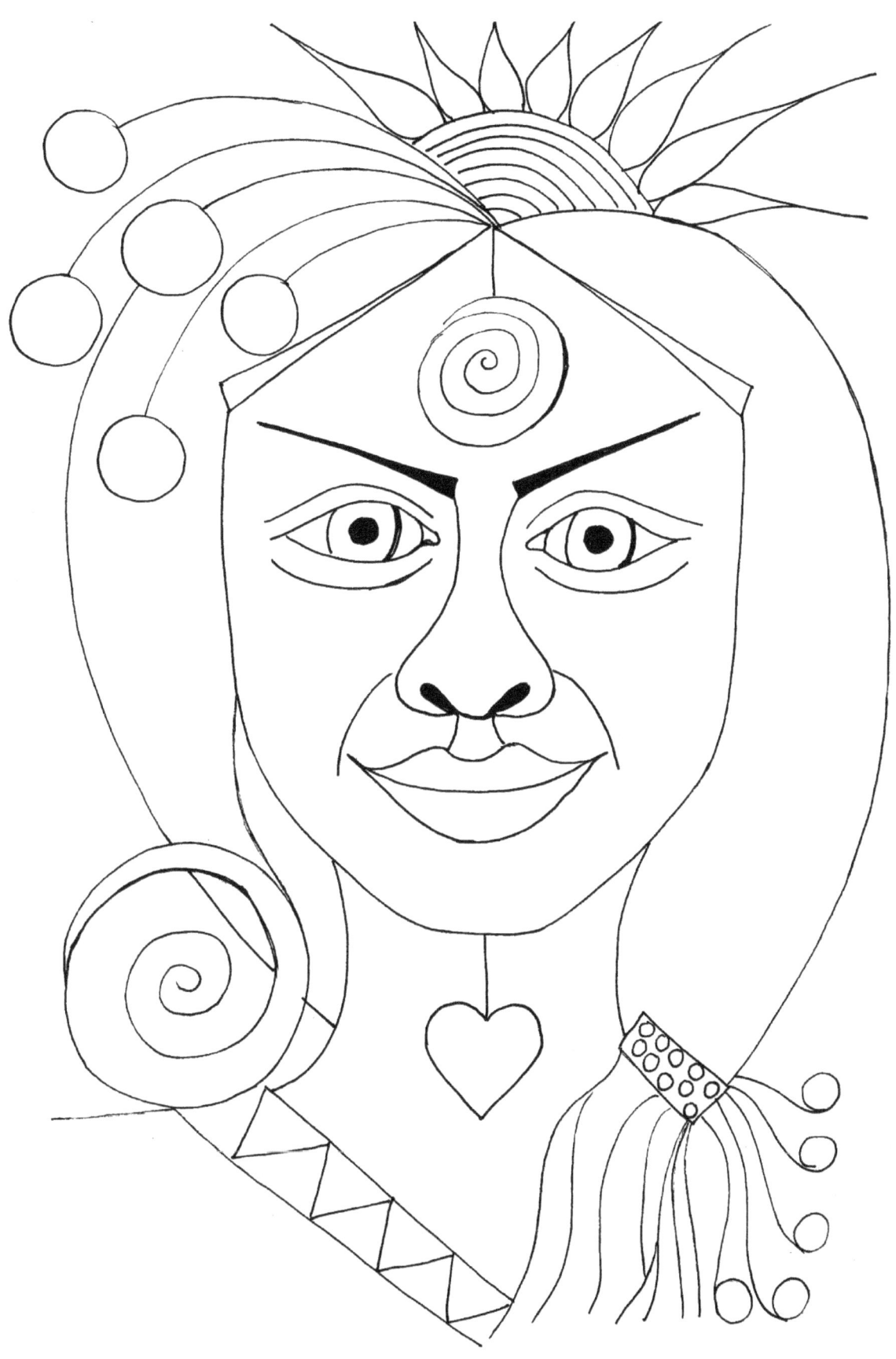

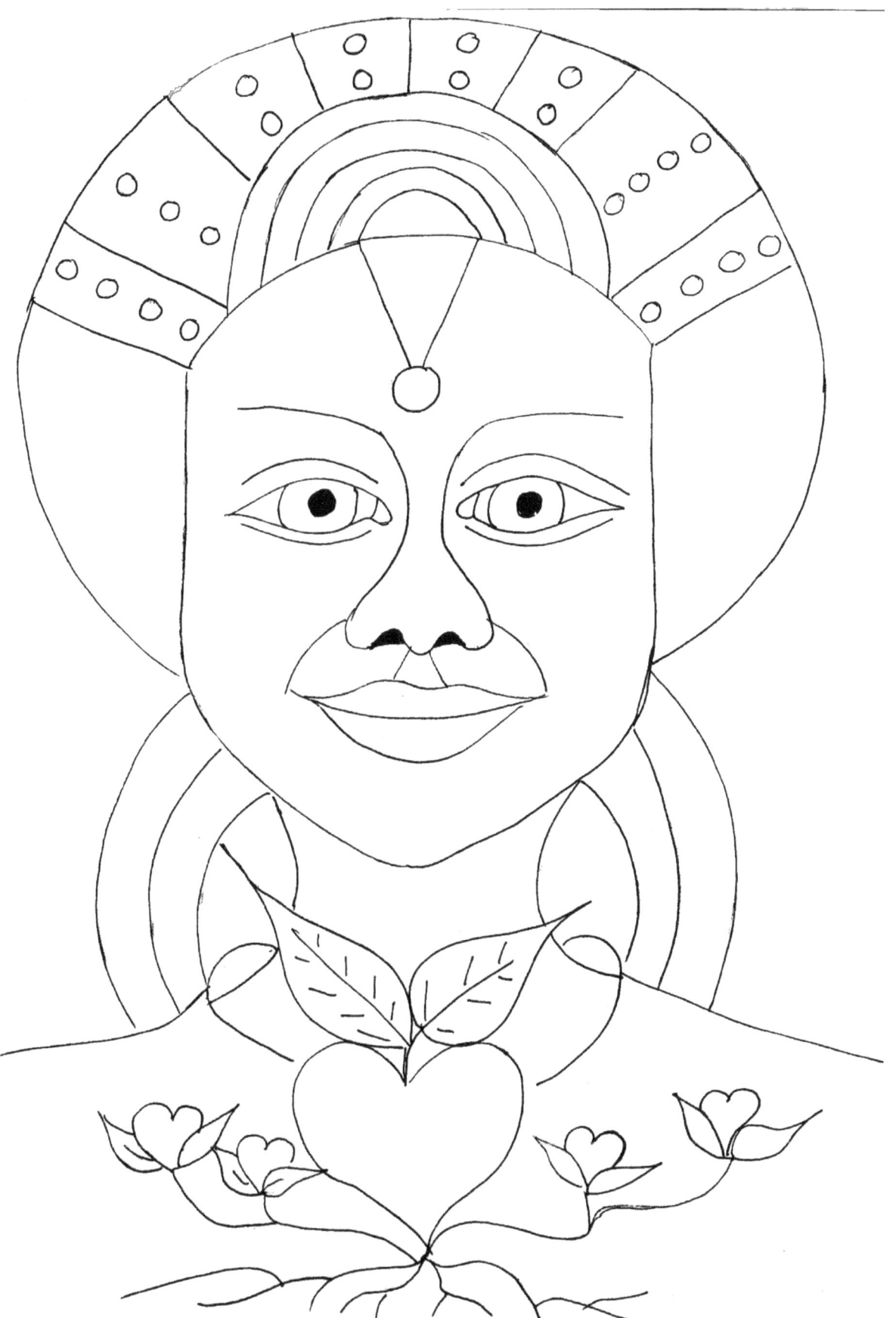

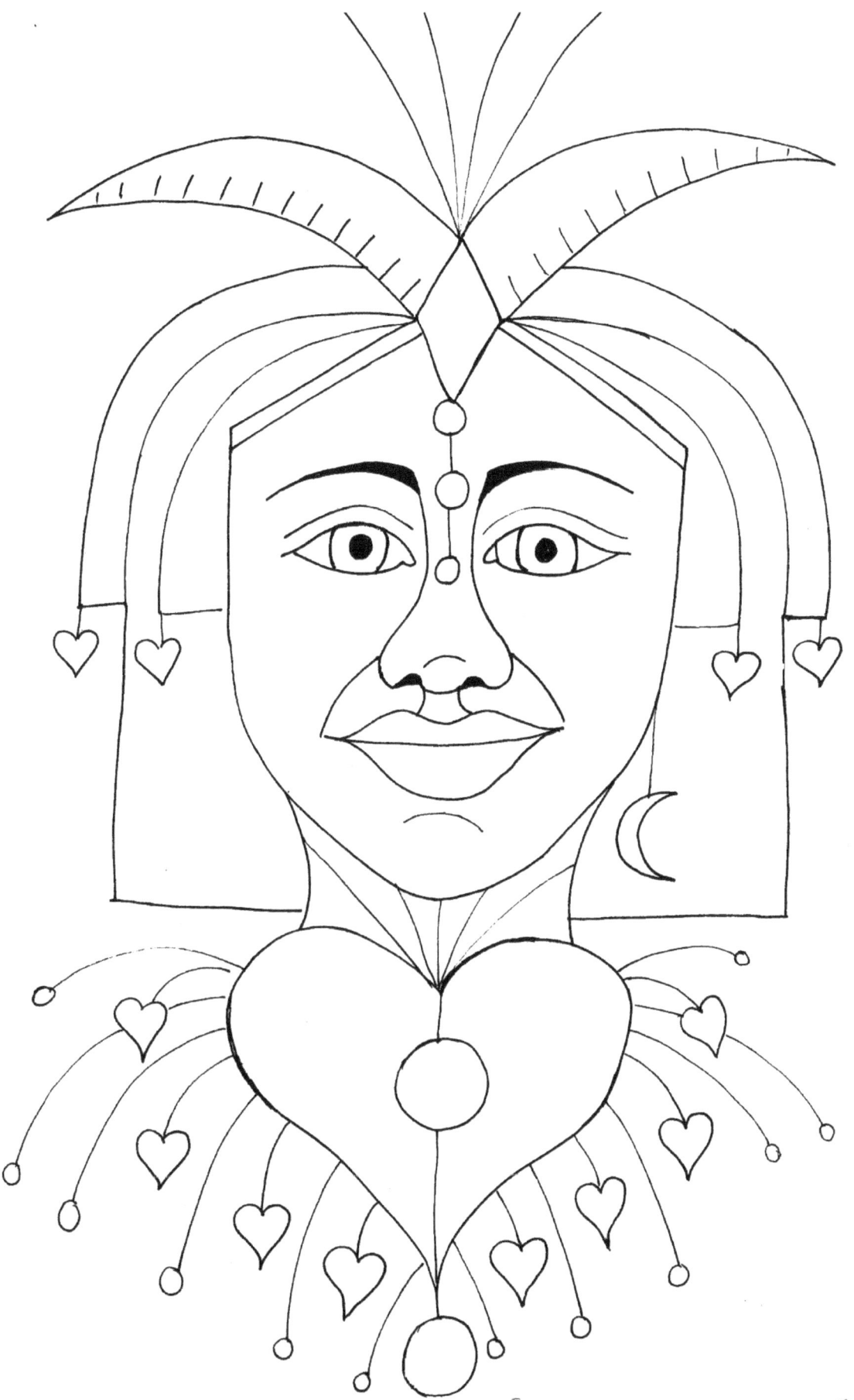

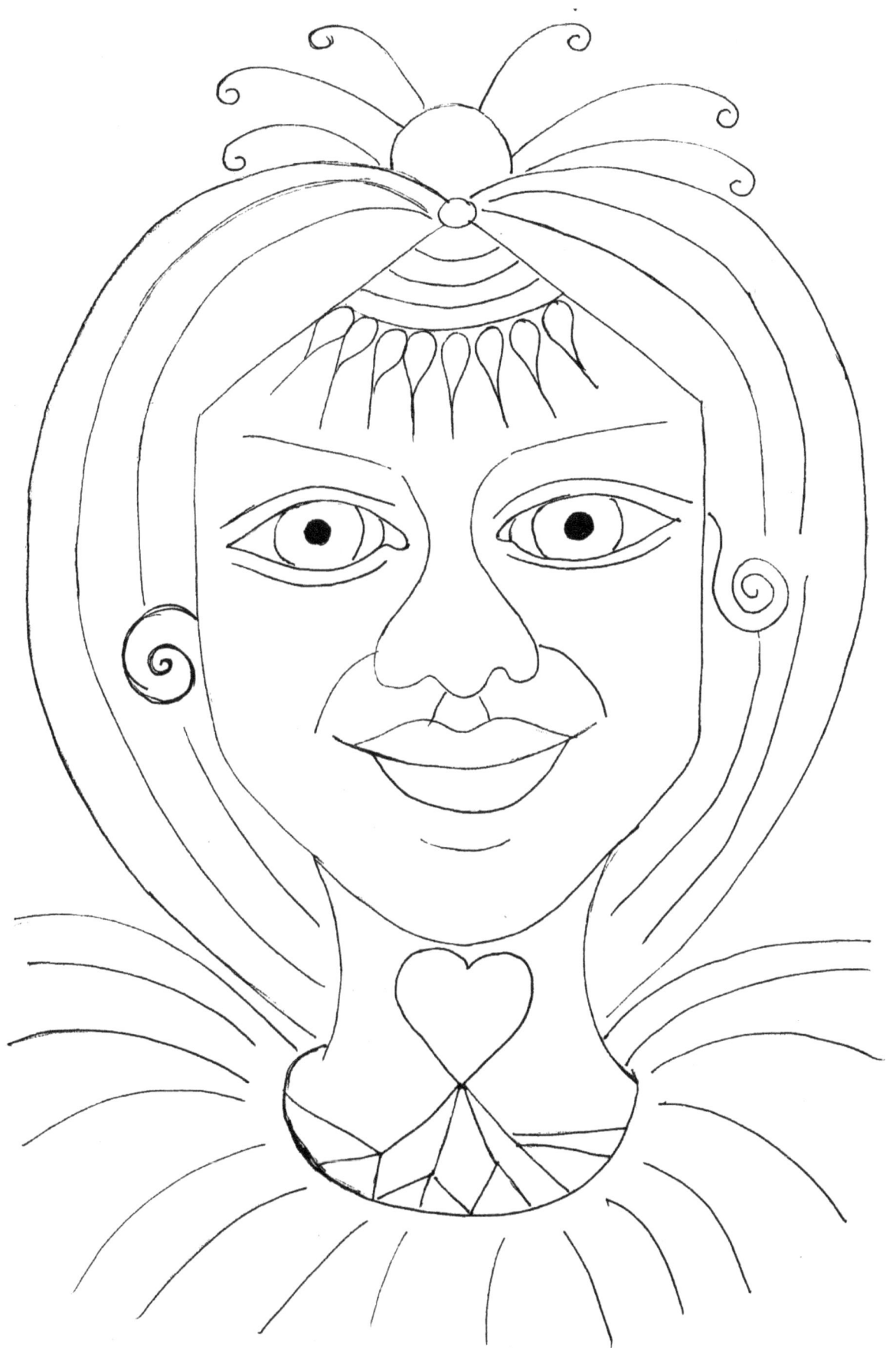

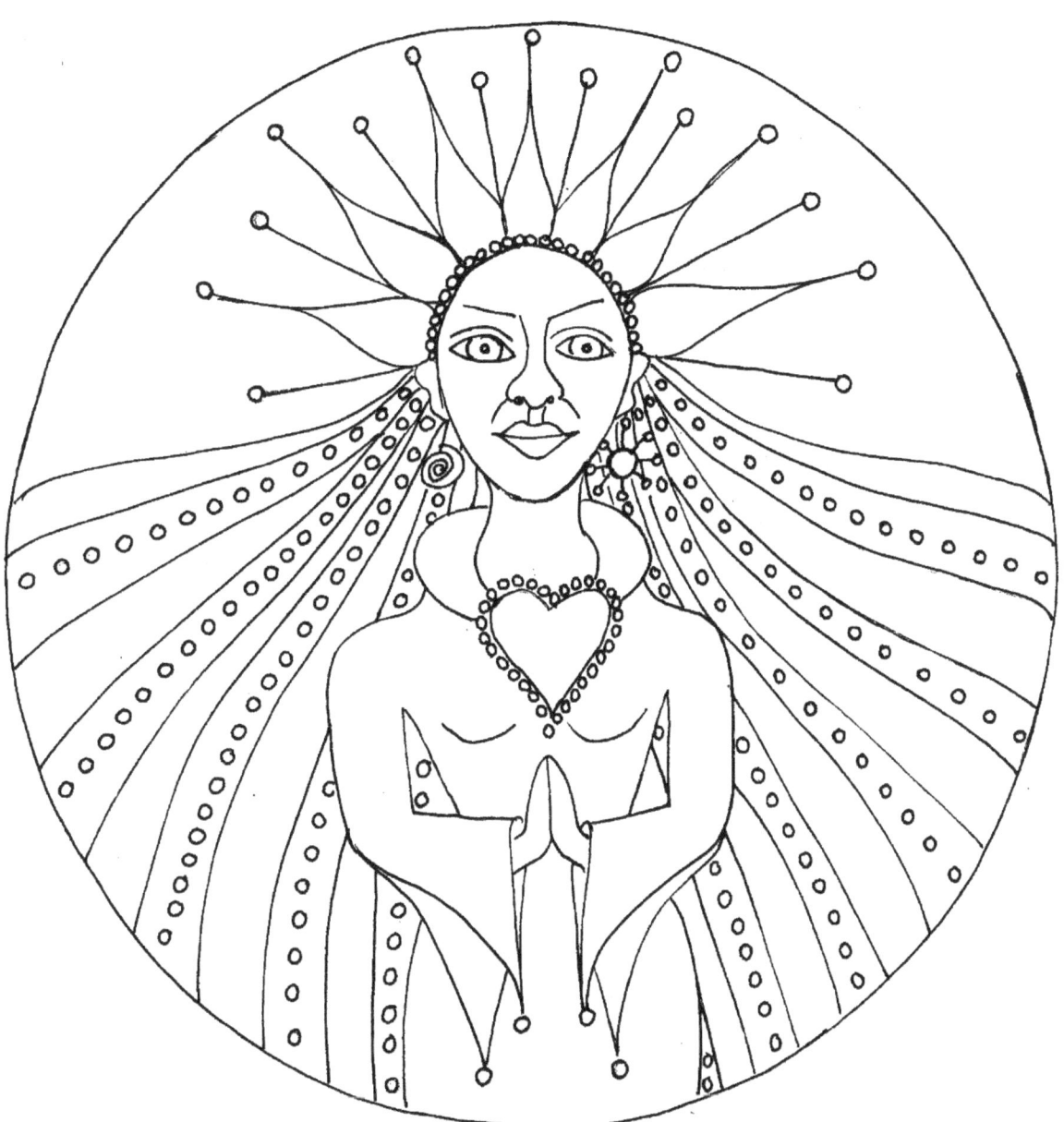

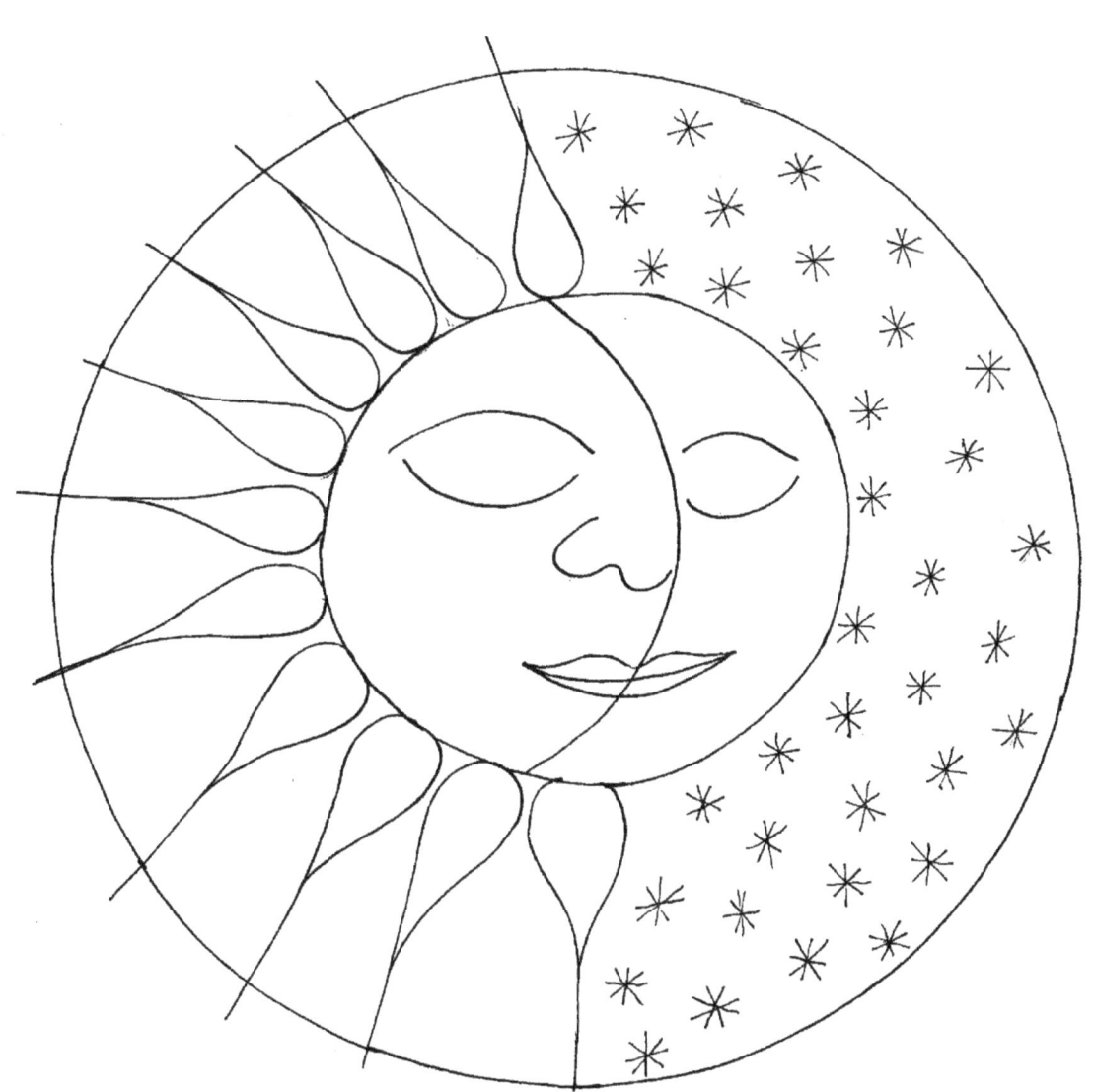

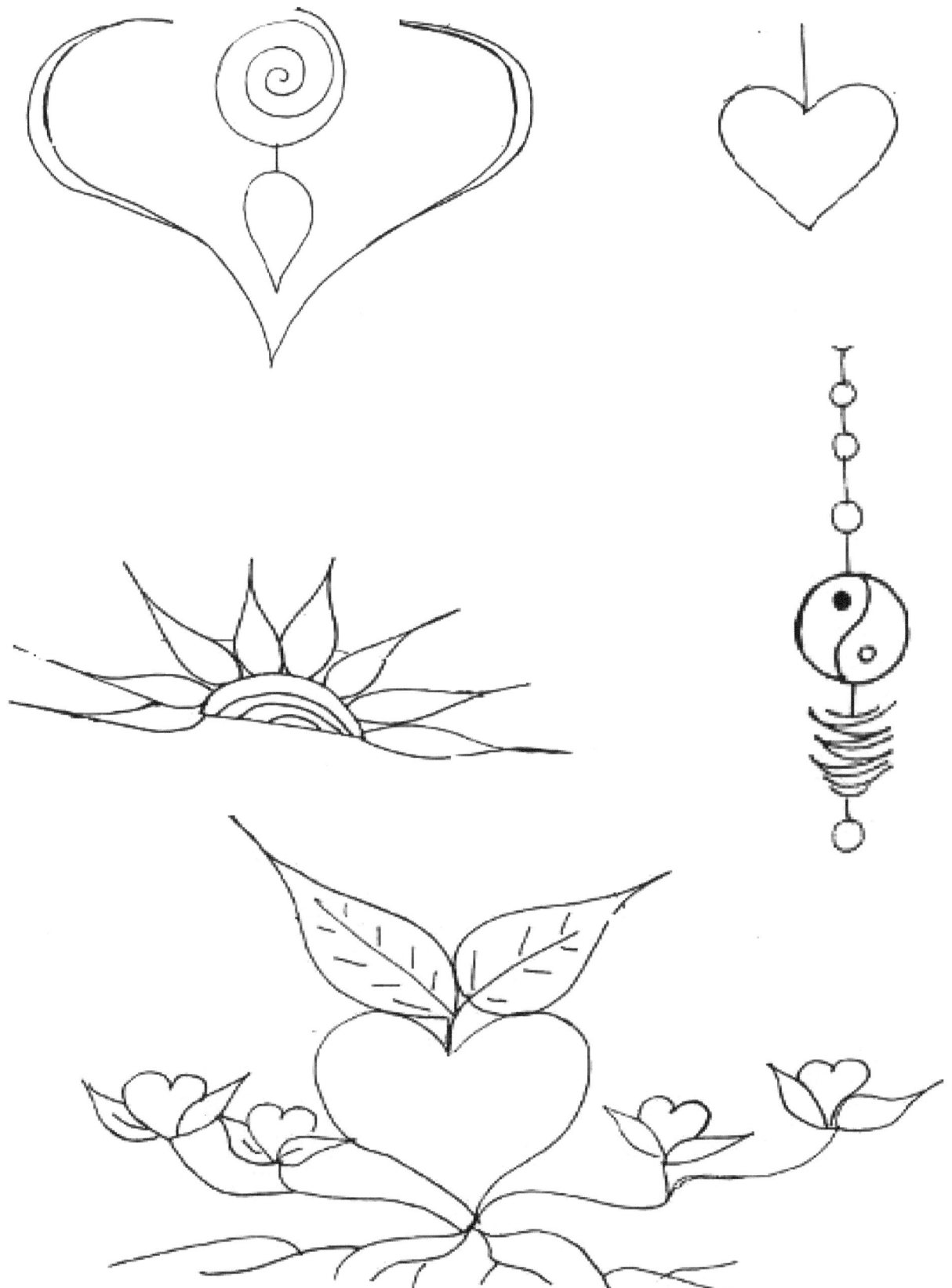

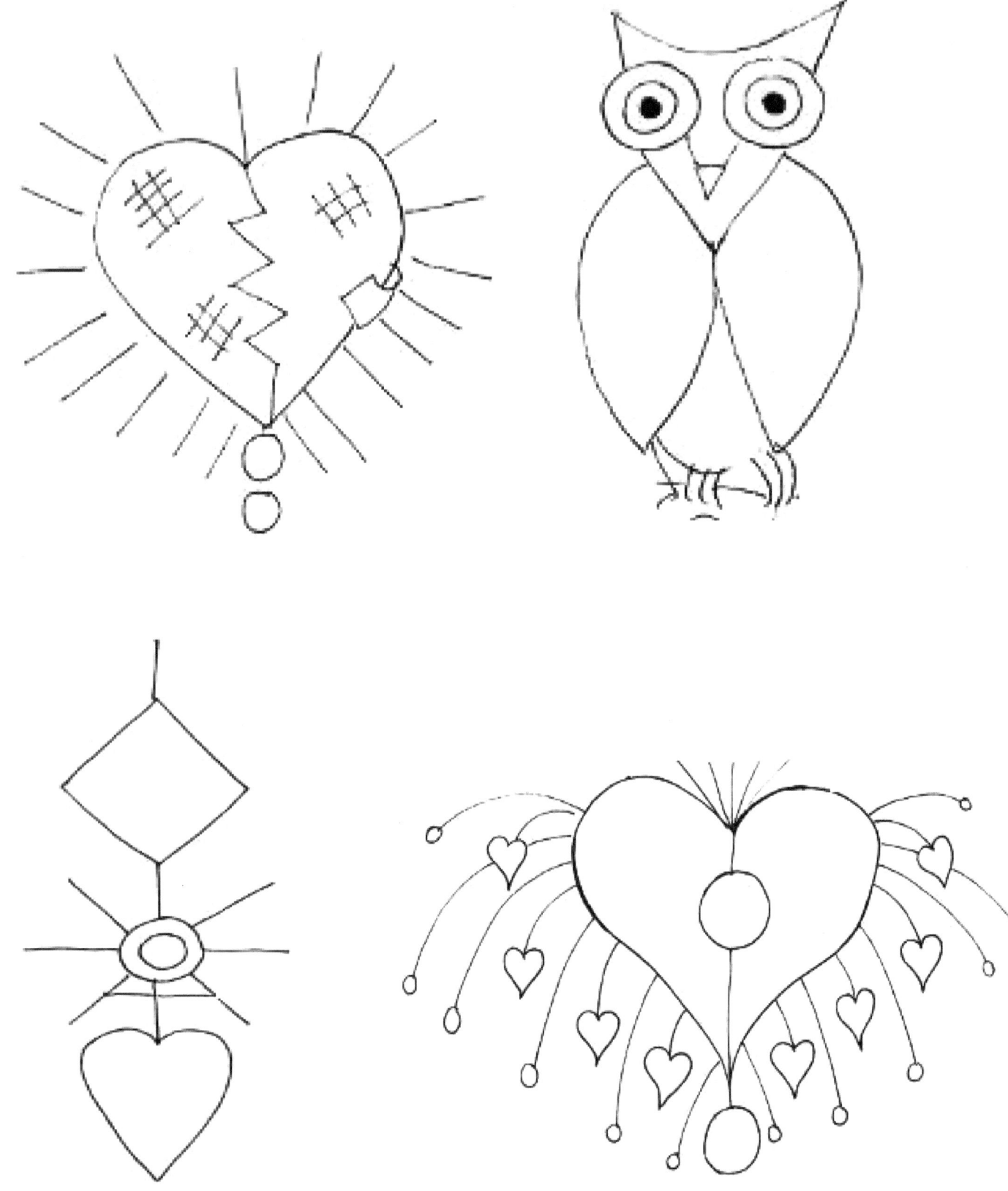

Journal about your experience:

....
....
....
....
....
....
....
....
....
....
....
....
....
....
....
....
....
....
....
....
....
....
....

Journal about your experience:

··

··

··

··

··

··

··

··

··

··

··

··

··

··

··

··

··

··

··

··

··

··

Journal about your experience:

....

....

....

....

....

....

....

....

....

....

....

....

....

....

....

....

....

....

....

....

....

....

Journal about your experience:

....

....

....

....

....

....

....

....

....

....

....

....

....

....

....

....

....

....

....

....

....

....

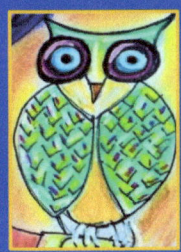

About the Author and Spiritual Teacher: Alessandra Del Basso as all
"Inner Wise Warriors" has experienced a life of challenges and is aware of the
many times she has fallen into the "Shadow" side. This however brought her
to start a search that would bring her to create "Rapport" with her shadow
sides and "SEE" the way to use this energy to fuel her journey rather than
hinder it. As she drew this information out of the fabric of the Universal
knowledge it also showed her the purpose of her life.

The Author's Life Purpose statement:

"I empower myself, so I can empower others and together we

transform the Planet, and we all prosper"

This "Spiritual Colouring Book reflects "passion" the author experiences
along her path. It is the path of light towards a more "creative" life and
aims to invite you to see in your life the power of the
"Inner Creativity".
"Be the Creator of your life not the "slave" of your mind!!"

I Trust you Enjoyed the Journey☺

Till next time